Designed by Flowerpot Press
www.FlowerpotPress.com
CHC-0909-0448
ISBN: 978-1-4867-1485-8
Made in China/Fabriqué en Chine

HOW DO BRIDGES NOT FALL DOWN?

A BOOK ABOUT ARCHITECTURE & ENGINEERING

written by jennifer shand

illustrated by srimalie bassani

ROMAN ARCH

impost

pier

EIFFEL TOWER

GOLDEN GATE BRIDGE

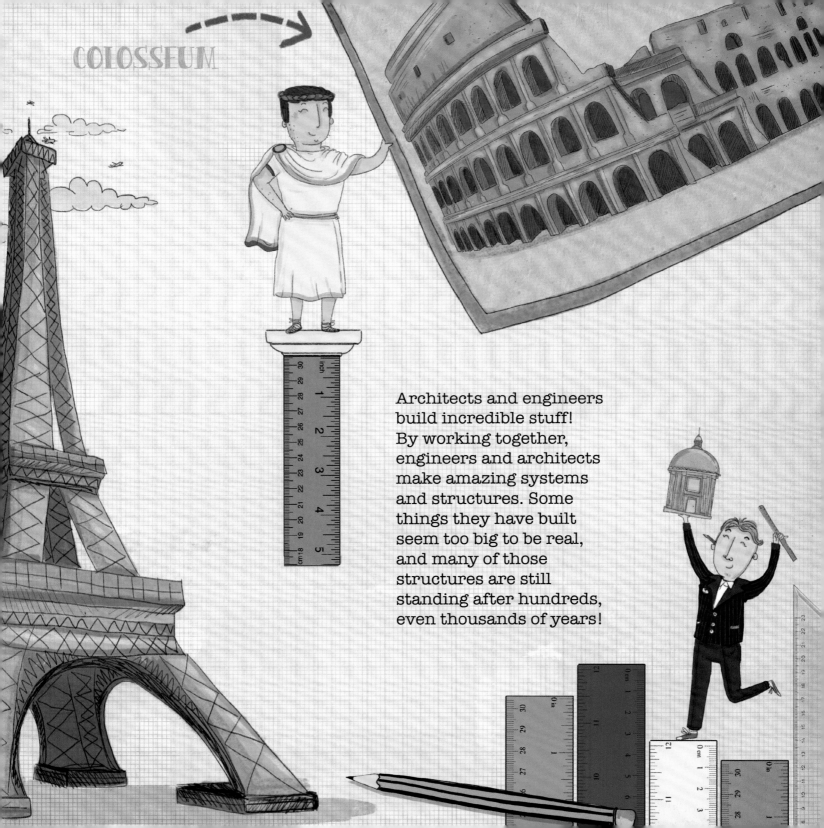

COLOSSEUM

Architects and engineers
build incredible stuff!
By working together,
engineers and architects
make amazing systems
and structures. Some
things they have built
seem too big to be real,
and many of those
structures are still
standing after hundreds,
even thousands of years!

How do bridges not fall down?
Are they all secretly sitting on magic carpets
that help them float?

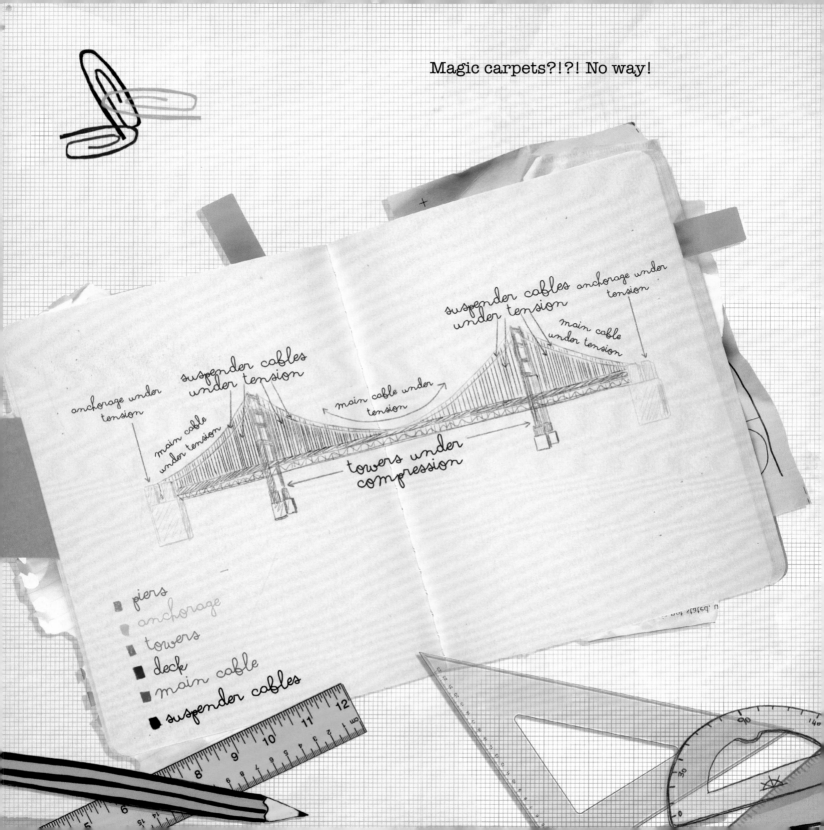

Magic carpets?!?! No way!

Bridges do not fall down because of the clever way they have been designed. There are actually many different types of bridges, and each one has a special system that keeps it from falling. One example of a bridge design is a suspension bridge, which is often used for long bridges like the Golden Gate Bridge in San Francisco. That bridge is 8,981 feet (2,737 meters) long!

A suspension bridge hangs the deck, which in many cases is the road, on cables that are suspended between towers. The towers hold most of the weight because the downward pressure on the deck travels up the cables to the towers. The towers then carry that pressure down to the foundation which supports the bridge.

How do boats move from one water level to another?

Do they take an elevator?

An elevator?!?! No way! Well, sort of...

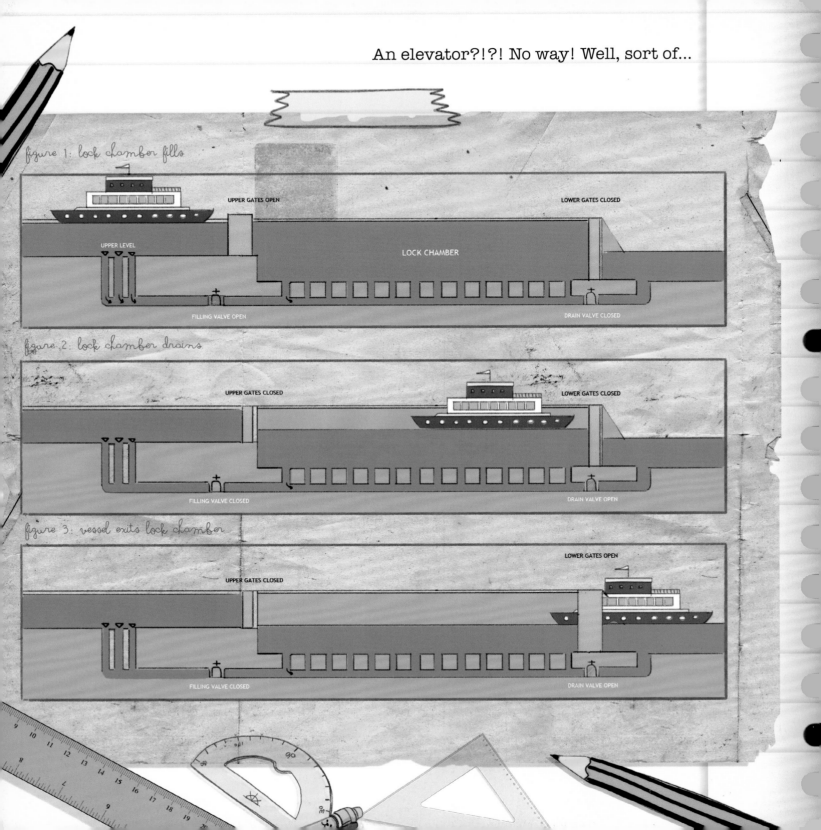

figure 1: lock chamber fills

UPPER GATES OPEN

LOWER GATES CLOSED

UPPER LEVEL

LOCK CHAMBER

FILLING VALVE OPEN

DRAIN VALVE CLOSED

figure 2: lock chamber drains

UPPER GATES CLOSED

LOWER GATES CLOSED

FILLING VALVE CLOSED

DRAIN VALVE OPEN

figure 3: vessel exits lock chamber

LOWER GATES OPEN

UPPER GATES CLOSED

FILLING VALVE CLOSED

DRAIN VALVE OPEN

Many water transportation routes use a lock system to move ships and barges up or down to meet the height of the next body of water. The boats go into the lock, which is a big chamber of water with gates at both ends. Then the boat waits while a valve is opened and water flows in (to raise the boat) or flows out (to lower the boat) until it matches the height of the water where the boat wants to go next. At that point, the gates on the lock open for the boat to continue on its way. So it is sort of like a boat elevator made from water!

How does a column and beam structure support all the weight that is above it?

Does it secretly ask a bunch of big gorillas to help hold everything up?

Gorillas?!?! No way!

The system of building that uses columns and beams has been around for over 5,000 years! In this system of construction, the load from above is transferred through the beam into the supporting columns and through the columns down to the foundation. Engineers and architects have to consider many factors when designing these systems, including the span between columns, the weight of the column and beam structure, and the load atop the structure.

COLUMN AND BEAM STRUCTURE

width

load

span

depth

beam

column

How do ancient buildings last so long?
Did builders cast spells on them to keep them
standing for thousands of years?

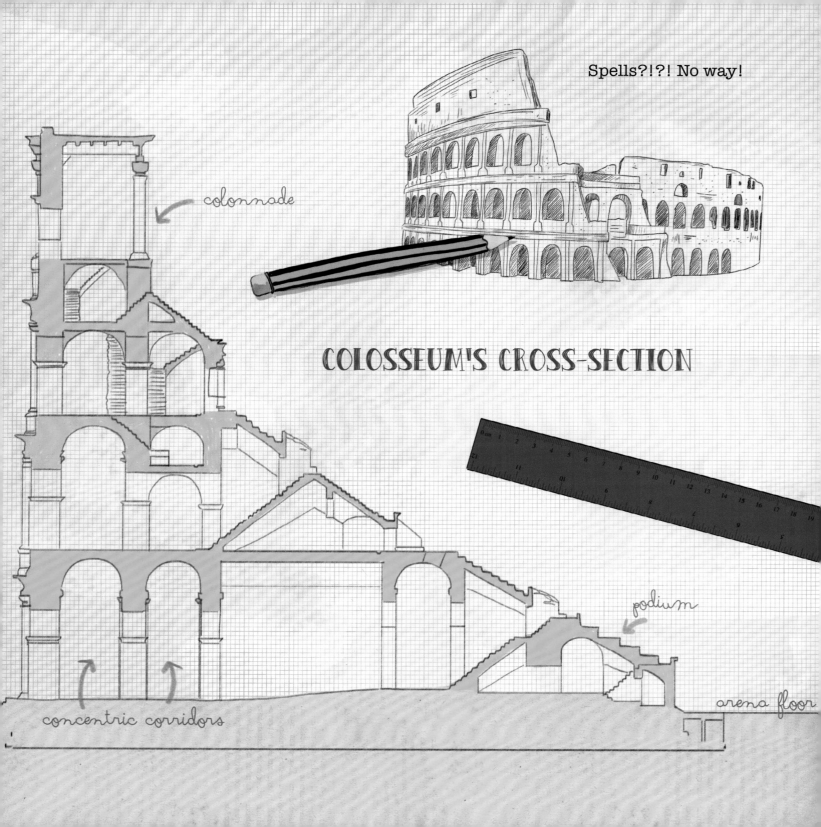

Spells?!?! No way!

colonnade

COLOSSEUM'S CROSS-SECTION

podium

concentric corridors

arena floor

One big reason that determines how long buildings last is how well they are designed. There are a variety of building methods that have stood the test of time. One example is the Colosseum in Rome, Italy.

The Colosseum is a massive four-level structure built by the Romans over 2,000 years ago. Part of the reason such a large structure has lasted so long is because the Romans invented a building method that uses arches in the design. Arches distribute the weight above each arch along their curve, which then rests on the supporting columns. The resulting weight of each floor is less than if they had built without arches, so the foundation has had to carry less weight through the years. This genius distribution of weight is one example of how design techniques have allowed builders to make big, strong buildings that last.

How do skyscrapers not tip over?
Is it because they work out every night to stay strong?

Work out?!?! No way!

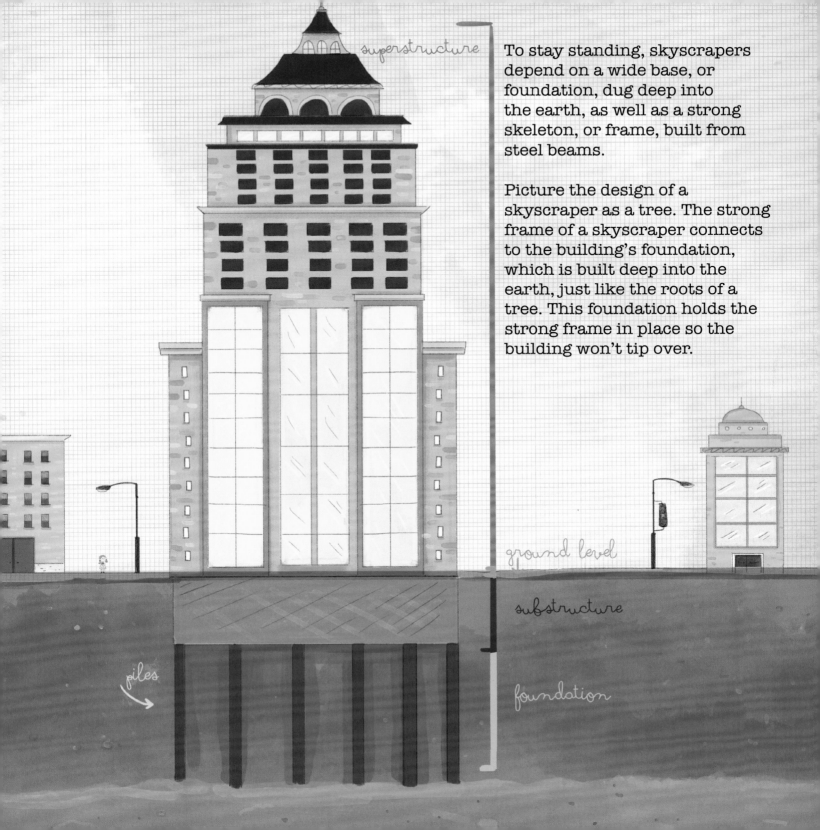

superstructure

To stay standing, skyscrapers depend on a wide base, or foundation, dug deep into the earth, as well as a strong skeleton, or frame, built from steel beams.

Picture the design of a skyscraper as a tree. The strong frame of a skyscraper connects to the building's foundation, which is built deep into the earth, just like the roots of a tree. This foundation holds the strong frame in place so the building won't tip over.

ground level

substructure

piles

foundation

NORTH AMERICA

SOUTH AMERICA

Why do buildings look so different
in different parts of the world?
Is it because they dress up to fit in?

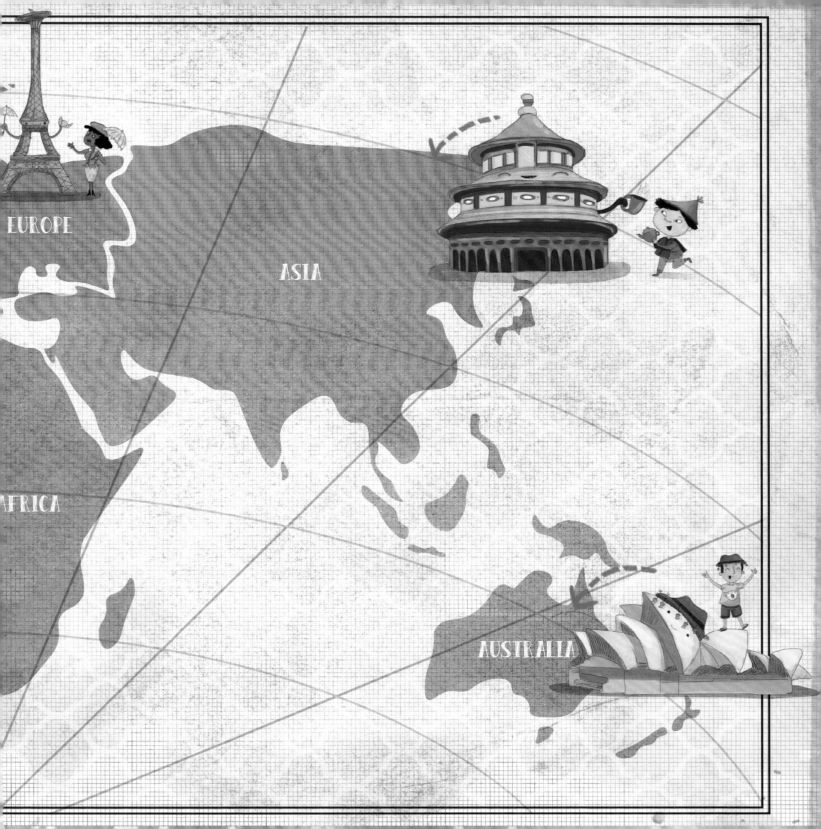

EUROPE

ASIA

AFRICA

AUSTRALIA

Dress up?!?! No way! Well, sort of...

COLOSSEUM

EIFFEL TOWER

PAGODA

PYRAMIDS

All around the world and all throughout our history, architects and engineers have used many different kinds of materials and many different building methods. What to build and how to build has been determined by a variety of factors.

One consideration when deciding what to build is how a building will fit into its surroundings. Other factors include: what building methods are known, what the climate is like, and what materials are available. Materials have included stone, wood, cement, mud, straw, and even snow!

Who knows what we will learn to build in the future?

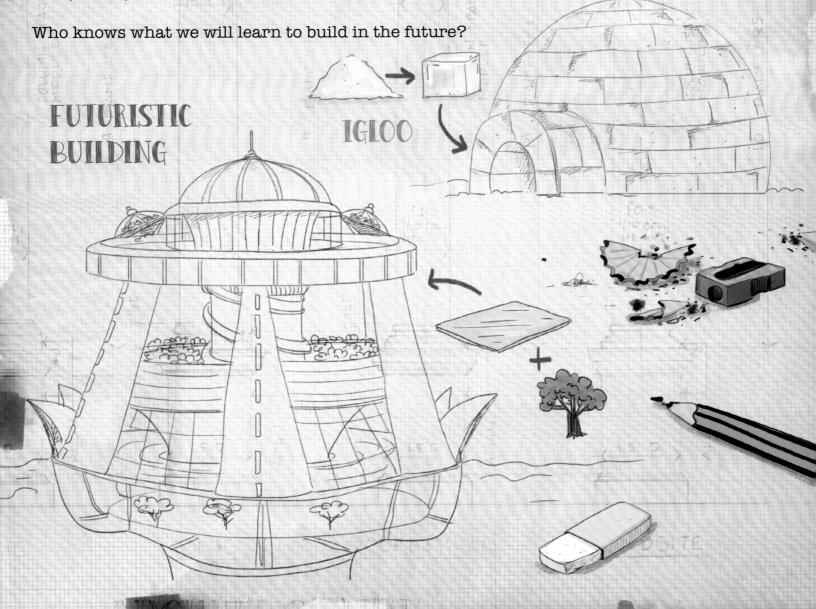

FUTURISTIC BUILDING

IGLOO

BRIDGES: Did you know there are six main types of bridges?

The Forth Bridge in Edinburgh, Scotland, is a **CANTILEVER** bridge, which means it is only supported on one end and uses either simple beams or steel trusses to hold it up.

The Henderson Waves bridge in Singapore is a **BEAM** bridge and consists of two towers and a single board across the top.

The Stone Arch bridge in Minneapolis, Minnesota, is an **ARCH** bridge, which means it is made of columns connected by arches.

The Tokyo Gate Bridge in Tokyo, Japan, is a **TRUSS** bridge, which is reinforced with metal poles that form a pattern around the deck.

The Millau Viaduct in Millau, France, is a **CABLE-STAYED** bridge and has one or more towers with cables that run along the sides to support the deck.

The Golden Gate Bridge in San Francisco, California, is a **SUSPENSION** bridge, which uses vertical cables to support the deck.

LOCKS: Did you know that some locks are able to move several boats at a time?

ENTRANCE GATE

LOCK

The world's two largest locks, Kieldrecht Lock and the Berendrecht Lock, are both located at the Port of Antwerp in Flanders, Belgium.

COLUMNS AND BEAMS: Did you know that Greek architects created three types of columns that are still used today?

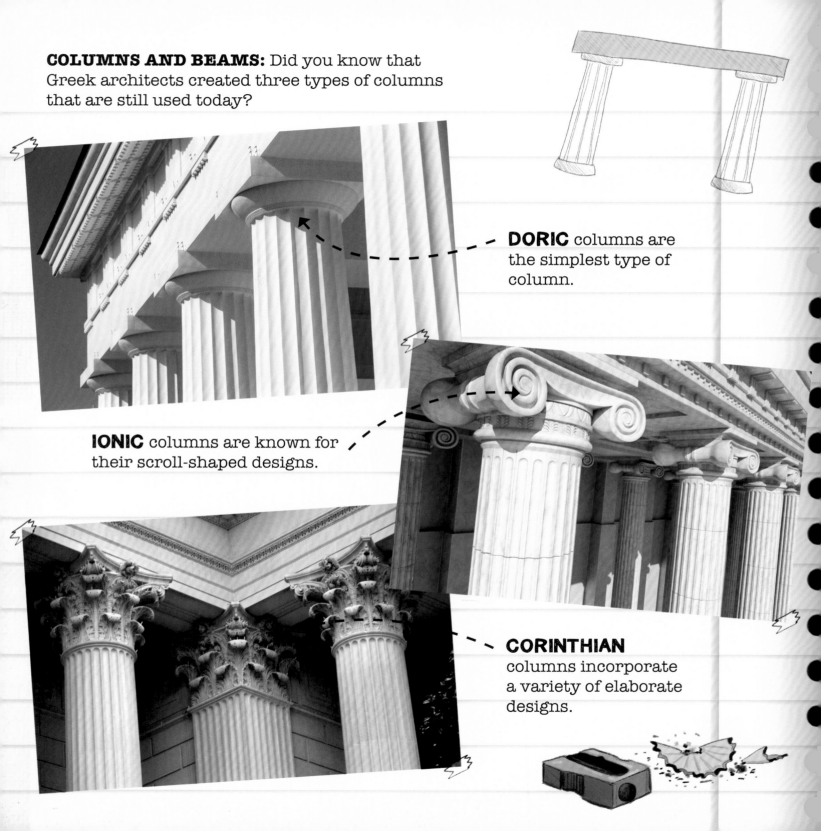

DORIC columns are the simplest type of column.

IONIC columns are known for their scroll-shaped designs.

CORINTHIAN columns incorporate a variety of elaborate designs.

ANCIENT BUILDINGS: Did you know that the Romans are credited for inventing a form of concrete that has helped keep their buildings standing tall for over 2,000 years?

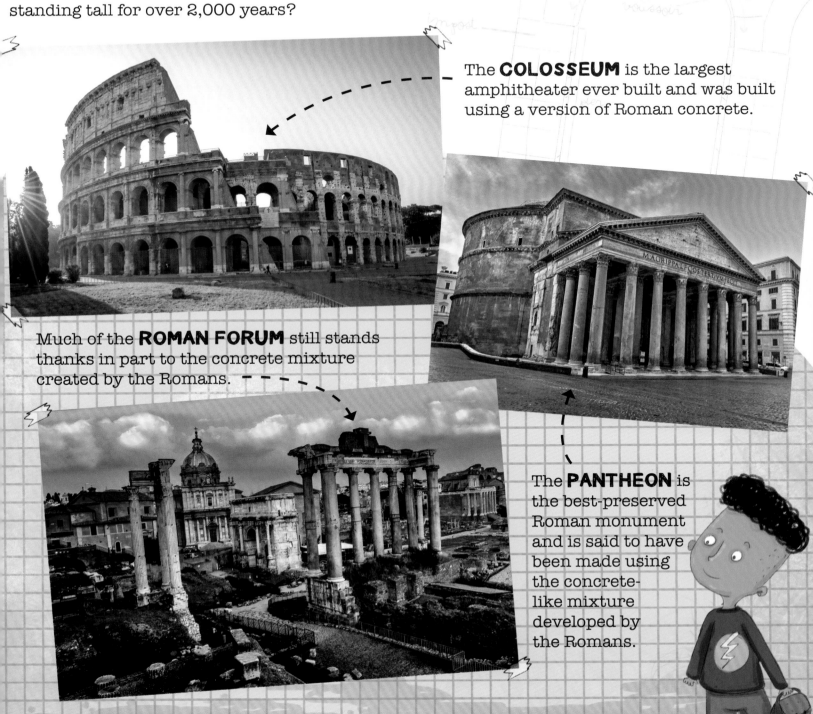

The **COLOSSEUM** is the largest amphitheater ever built and was built using a version of Roman concrete.

Much of the **ROMAN FORUM** still stands thanks in part to the concrete mixture created by the Romans.

The **PANTHEON** is the best-preserved Roman monument and is said to have been made using the concrete-like mixture developed by the Romans.

SKYSCRAPERS: Did you know that the three tallest skyscrapers in the world are all taller than 1,900 feet (579 meters)?

MAKKAH CLOCK ROYAL TOWER
Mecca, Saudi Arabia
1,972 feet
(601 meters)

BURJ KHALIFA
Dubai, United Arab Emirates
2,717 feet
(828 meters)

SHANGHAI TOWER
Shanghai, China
2,073 feet
(632 meters)

BUILDING STYLES: Did you know buildings around the world have been specially designed to withstand weather and other natural elements?

Some Chinese architecture incorporates a 2,500-year-old system of wooden brackets called "**DOUGONG**" on roofs of buildings to help them withstand earthquakes.

The Inuit people of Greenland and Canada developed **IGLOOS**, or shelters made of blocks of snow, to protect themselves from deadly blizzards and icy temperatures.

The **EIFFEL TOWER** was expertly designed to withstand winds in Paris, France, up to 155 mph (250 km/h).